This Wild Dance

S.R. Hardy

Für Annika. Ich liebe dich.

Contents

This Wild Dance

This Wild Dance

Muddy paths
And streams like veins of blood
Wind their way among the trees,
Both green-topped towers
And dying husks of gray and brown,
Gifting us this walk,
This glimpse of life,
This wild dance.

Wheeling Northward

Seven geese, wheeling northward,
Freed from earth
But sensing its power,
A subtle line below.

Two bluebirds at the roadside
Leap, in a simple flutter,
From ground to branch,
And rest
Between the worlds.

Two paths,
Two routes to freedom,
Two duties to perform:
One a sermon and the other a rite.

Death is a Mountain

Death is a mountain,
Breaking the sky.

The weight of its rocks
Drive down the earth,
Crushing life
And the tricks of wealth and strength;
It crushes all but the fame of deeds.

A Living Labyrinth

Branches tent the path,

Crowning the darkness

Of the forest's heart,

Leading us on,

Inward,

Until we wander

Lost

Among the trees:

A living labyrinth.

The Cold Sun of March

The cold sun of March

Reveals the creases on my face,

Daughters of time,

Scars and ridges

Like mountains and valleys,

The map and territory

Of my life.

No Mountains Anymore

No mountains anymore,
Just towers;
Concrete and steel
With offices, not caves.

No groves anymore,
Just alleys of garbage and glass;
Home to the homeless;
The sacred long fled.

No ocean anymore,
Nothing to be crossed,
No worlds to find.

Death Card

Our years hold many deaths,

A series of bloody dismemberments.

We float above

And look at the shambles,

At the blood and the bone,

And dream of what we might become.

First Snow

Diamonds rain down to earth,
Shattered clouds
Glittering as they fall,
Each perfect,
Each frozen,
Encasing a world,
A universe of being
From lake to mountain
And forest to sky;
Each world unique,
Perfect,
Complete.

What Exists is Fire, All-Consuming

What exists is fire,
All-consuming.
It fills the world
Within and without;
A threefold drive
Towards heat and light
And life itself.

At End of Day Before the Dark

At end of day
Before the dark
The greens and browns
And reddish hues
Hold back the mist
That grows and grows,
Ruthless as the night.

Snorri

Like Snorri, I am *here*,
A hermit longing for home,
Alone in a forest
With pages for trees,
Where the gods are a river
And my mind is a salmon
Lunging upstream.

A Timeless Fire

Berries swell with life

Like blood from the earth,

A timeless fire,

Bright and dripping

With beads of water:

Daughters of the drizzle.

A Hint of Farther Heavens

Hammer-filled thoughts,

Echoes of thunder,

Roar through my head

Then freeze,

Fixed in the sky,

Poised to strike

Like summer lightning:

A hint of farther heavens.

As Dark Comes Down

As dark comes down
I walk the path,
Heavened by branches
And fateless sky.

The earth cracks open;
A scent arises
Of mud and trees
And flowing water.

From nose to blood;
The forest fills me
With knowledge of trees,
Ancient and hard.

Or Sink in the Trying

Dark tree over water;
Mirrorsky and ripples for clouds,
The sun a sinking pebble
In inky vastness.

Light on the shore,
A beacon for daring:
Swim to the light
Or sink in the trying.

The Vicious Instant

The gods are furrows
Dug in the brain.
Each is unique,
Born of the vicious instant
Of carving
Awaiting seed, sun and water.

Three Yews for Samhaintide

Oldest is truest when it comes to tales,

The whisper in the darkness

We try not to hear.

Sometimes

We hear it in our bones,

A humming like bees:

Ancient, ill-formed and dark.

The Gods Flow Forward

The gods flow forward
Driven by lack,
A piercing urge
That wombs the world,
Sowing their seed
And calling forth
Both sun and water.

The Law, the Wheel and Time

To know life is to know
The winds and tides
And the turning of the seasons,
The leaves as they fall
And the sprouts as they grow.

To know life is to know
The Law, the Wheel and Time.

Last Snow

It falls to earth,

Wandering

Downward and northward,

Covering ground both green and brown,

Scraped and torn by winter's claw.

Then it rests,

Melting into the earth.

Winter's Dream

The earth swallowed me,
Soft flesh and hard bone
Sinking slowly,
Collapsing inwards
Like hope
Or a flower in winter.
The earth covered me,
Protecting me,
Charging me with life:
It readied me for spring.

Dusk Occidental

Dusk occidental
Swarms the horizon:
Slow collapse and long descent.
The darkness is a doom raven,
Its feathers cushion the fall.

At Rest, I Can Read the World

At rest, I can read the world,
Let it come to me,
Above and Below.

I can open my eyes
And see
Future and past;
Tathagata.

I am *jafna*,
Ready to leap
Across the abyss
When I start tilting.

I wear my *hamingja*,
My *fylgja*, my forbears and line,
Like a cloak without seams.

I understand trees,
The flight of birds
And the bark of dogs.

At rest, I can read the world.

Half-Blind Snake

The sky comes down
As I burst from the earth,
A half-blind snake
Wrapped in swaddling clouds:
Divine embrace.
Beating wings fill my head,
Whirring;
The song halves,
One side ecstasy
And the other fear.

The Yieldless Wheel

I am thronged by life
And thronged by death,
Jostled, jumbled and clashing
With Nature herself,
Great Mother,
Fearsome in strength,
In age and in wisdom;
Mother of sky,
Mother of earth
And of the wheel
That turns without yielding.

Endless Underworld

New birds in the old sky;

New morning.

Thousand-year sky;

An endless underworld.

The flight of birds is a world logos:

Speech for those with ears,

Wisdom for those with hearts.

Summer's End

At summer's end,

The Mórrígan sings,

Howling like a wolf with spears for teeth;

Winter's song,

The Mórrígan's gift;

Sickness, old age and death:

The long hard night.

If a Rose Were a Mountain

If a rose were a mountain
It would bloom forever;
Eternal unfolding,
Always now,
Timeless and rooted
Deep in the earth.
If a mountain were a rose
It would rise each spring,
Pushing skyward;
Snowy heaven.
Then it would sink
Every fall,
Steadily lower,
Toothless and old,
Back to the earth
To wait.

There Is a River

There is a river,

Bornless, deathless,

Swelling the sky,

Dropping to earth

To wash the mountains

And cut its way down to the valleys

To water the fields,

Sinking into the earth,

Then rising,

Reborn

As a wonderful mist,

Back to the sky,

The sea of air.

Boudicca's Lament

Roman power,
Thrusting north,
Razed the land,
The people's soul.
Bloody wings of empire
Stretched across the seas,
Coveting the earth and siring
Beautiful bastards, but torn.

The Sun's Companion

Full moon rising,

Burning through the darkness

And cloaked in clouds,

Useless fetters for the sun's companion;

Rising in the east,

Hunted by the light.

Samhain Moon

The moon sits low
Above the trees,
Above the world;
The light in the darkness,
The All in the Nothing;
A hint of the truth:
Everything that was will be again.

Becomes a Vastness

Two hearts together twined
Beget a third and then the many;
All one,
But a Oneness ever smaller,
Until its smallness
Becomes a vastness,
Unseen, profound.

The Archer and the Arrow Nocked

In the forest,
When green fades to black,
I sight my prey
Through an arc of yew.
Then in a flashing leap
It is gone,
Running to its home
And I am alone,
Seeing myself through trees' eyes;
Taut and wary.

Then I ask myself:
If I am the archer
What is the arrow?

Forsythia, First to Bloom

Forsythia,

First to bloom;

A rush of yellow,

A riot of color,

A wave of youth

Both bright and bold,

Surging to meet

The sunshine of spring.

March

Hope rides the wind,
Raw and scraping.

Melted snow mingles
With muddy soil.

Seeds await
Spring's first blooming
Under thawing earth.

Holy Silver, Son of Gold

With time
The woods grow darker.
With time
They grow twisted and thick,
Smothered and shadowed,
With only fleeting rays of moonlight,
Holy silver, son of gold,
To show the way.

November

November is for thinkers,
Cold, but not too cold
And early to dark.

A hint of death
Swirls in the air
Like leaves in the wind,
Deep and slow;
A funereal march.

Into Another

In the beginning we fall,

Downward and northward,

Hard and fast,

Endless down,

Tracked and unerring,

Shaking and humming.

And then comes the bend,

Blindly skewing,

Breaking the rule,

Crashing its neighbor;

One at first,

Then it turns

Into another,

Then two more,

Then three,

Then five,

Then eight,

Then three plus ten

And on and on

And on.

Elephants and Truth

I like old things,

Dark and bare and covered in dust,

Smelling of time,

Perfumed ghosts;

Known but ignored

Like elephants and truth.

A Time of No Time

Paradise is a time not a place,

A time of no time

When body and mind escape the fates

And rise,

Riding the wave of the world;

Above life,

Above death.

Pendragon

We are each a hollow hill,

An otherworld pregnant with treasure,

A holy mountain

Home to a dragon

Dreaming of flight:

A serpent in air,

Shimmering scales

In moonlight washed,

Belly to earth and back to sky,

As fire,

Holy fire,

Fills the horizon.

The Painted Abyss

We stand alone,
Children of earth
And boundless heaven,
That painted abyss,
That crushing weight
Of blue and white
With hints,
Only hints,
Of purple that are
Worn with shyness,
Like love confessed to a diary.

Cosmos

Sky fills the eye
With vastness;
Infinity pockmarked
By furious stars,
Ageless and burning.
Widest of wastes,
Nous and *stoff*,
Forever entwined.
It is the bornless cradle,
Known beyond sense:
Cosmos,
Nothing-not-nothing.

Alban Arthan

In the longest night, the year is born,
When the sun has died its little death;
The seed of fire, the flame of life,
Eternal *now* unfolding,
Lifts the weight of night and time,
Eating darkness,
Growing light.

Imbolc

Winter's night,
Swollen with dawn,
With life and with light.
Green seeds lie frozen
In darkness and ice,
Dreaming of earth
And the waxing of day.

Alban Eiler

Day and night
As equals matched,
Soil and sky lie waiting.
The sun rises,
Then plunges earthward;
The horizon swells,
Ready to burst.

Beltane

Fire in the mind,
Fire in the earth;
Seeds in the field
Straining for sun,
To remake the world,
New and pure.

Alban Hefin

Morning shouts and night whispers,
Soft and sleek.

But day,
Day sings, strong and fearless;
Child of the sun,
Beloved of the heavens.

Lughnasadh

Sun rides high,
Seeding Earth
With life and light.
Earth is robed in green and yellow,
Food for the belly,
Food for the mind.

Winter sleeps while life sings,
Dancing with joy;
The world-child.

Alban Elfed

Summer mourns the turning leaves,

Harvest's shadow

    -Death foretold-

Adorning the trees

Like jewels in the crown

Of a dying king;

Straining earthward,

Darkness and fire

Locked in embrace.

Samhain

The earth is robed in fallen leaves,
Gold, fire red and brown.

They sink,
Second by second
Into the earth.

Decay fills the air,
Thick and sweet
Like memories of youth.

Faith, Like a Plague

The ancient poets
Were friends of the gods,
Tellers of a truth
Like fresh-blown glass,
Young and supple,
Like man before the Fall,
The real one,
When dogma won the day
And faith, like a plague,
Entered our midst.

My Own Hermopolis

I have found the spot
But not yet the emerald,
Just a few broken pots
And various grave goods.
But I keep digging,
Looking for the City;
My own Hermopolis,
Full of temples
Mirrored to the sky:
All equal,
Thrice balanced,
Thrice great.

Weltenbaum

I hang, suspended,

Not of this world

But tethered to it

By indecisive magnetism.

I hang alone,

In perfect freedom,

Not superman but anarch,

Defiant but longing.

Five Gates for Knowing

The world fountain
is ever flowing;
Five streams for bathing
Veining the earth;
Five gates for knowing,
Opening to the world
As we are born,
Overrun and wailing.

The Way of Points

Fire,

Drawn to fire,

Pulls upwards

Towards the answer,

Yet deeper,

Always following

The spark of life.

Three Paths of a Seed

A seed has only three paths:

Downward
Into the earth,
Seeking water;

Upward
Into the sky,
Seeking sun;

And within,
Growing from the center;
Spiral after endless spiral.

Three Natures of a Word

A word has a threefold nature:

The word itself, blunt and raw,
A thing of force and power;

An image in the mind,
Shimmering with the joy of knowledge;

And purest meaning, without shape or sound,
The bridge between the All and the Nothing.

A Marriage is Like a Ruby

A marriage is like a ruby,

A precious rock

Both beautiful and constant,

Shot through with imperfections,

Iron rods

Turned by time

To silky threads of wisdom.

The All and the Nothing

The world is a fourness
Of crosses and squares,
And octagons;
Their flower.

The world is a threeness
Of triangles and arrows,
And hexagons;
Their diamond.

The world is a twoness,
Of Above and Below,
And balance;
Their rider.

The world is a oneness
Of the All,
And the Nothing;
Its shadow.

Watchers at the Well

Three ladies of fate,
Weird sisters,
Watch at the well;
The mother of time.
They are earth and air
To our lives,
Like the sea to a fish.

Metaphor

Both like and not,

A whispering bear,

It hangs before us,

The thinnest of veils,

Offering both distortion and truth.

Memory

Memory is a funhouse mirror,
Infinitely untrue in all directions,
A mocking fool mocking the fool
That stands before it
Empty handed,
Without a hammer
Or enough courage for a fist.